THE YOUNG PERSON'S GUIDE TO THE

Ballet

WITH MUSIC ON CD FROM *THE NUTCRACKER*,
SWAN LAKE, AND *THE SLEEPING BEAUTY*

THE YOUNG PERSON'S GUIDE TO THE

Ballet

WITH MUSIC ON CD FROM *THE NUTCRACKER,*
SWAN LAKE, AND *THE SLEEPING BEAUTY*

BOOK WRITTEN BY
ANITA GANERI

HARCOURT BRACE & COMPANY

SAN DIEGO   NEW YORK   LONDON

First published in Great Britain in 1998 by
PAVILION BOOKS LTD
London House, Great Eastern Wharf
Parkgate Road London sw11 4NQ

First U.S. edition 1998

Ballet consultant: Jane Pritchard
Designer: Nigel Partridge
Editor: Jo Fletcher-Watson
Picture Research: Amy McKay

Library of Congress Cataloging in-Publication Data
Ganeri. Anita, 1961–
The young person's guide to the ballet
with music on CD from *The Nutcracker, Swan Lake*,
and *The Sleeping Beauty*/book written by Anita Ganeri—1st U.S. ed.
p.   cm
Includes index
ISBN 0-15-201184-6
1. Ballet–Juvenile literature.   1. Title
GV1787.5.G36   1998
792.8–de21   97–3806

A C E F D B

Printed in China

Contents

Introduction

Enter the world of classical ballet and share in the magic of one of the world's most beautiful forms of dance! Though ballet dancers move with an enchanting grace, their light-footed ease is the result of years of hard work – and is part of a tradition that stretches back for centuries.

Peter Ilyich Tchaikovsky is considered a master of ballet music, and excerpts from his three balletic masterpieces – *The Nutcracker, Swan Lake,* and *The Sleeping Beauty* – are featured on the CD at the front of this book. But there is much more to ballet than Tchaikovsky, as you will discover in the pages that follow. Learn about ballet's history, from the early Romantic period to the Dance Theatre of Harlem's modern productions. Meet the legends of dance and take a look backstage at the choreographers, costume and stage designers, and other invaluable contributors. Follow a dancer from his or her first steps in a classroom to a flawless *pas de deux* in a production of a modern ballet company. And find out why ballet has thrilled generations – and is now more popular than ever before.

(left) The christening scene from the opening act of The Sleeping Beauty

What Is Ballet?

Welcome to the ballet! As the audience falls silent and the orchestra strikes up, the curtain rises on a magical scene. The beauty of the dancers and the grandeur of the music transport the audience to another world.

What is ballet?

The Snowflakes from Act I of The Nutcracker

Ballet uses music and dance instead of words to tell a story. Sometimes the story is a well-known tale, such as *The Sleeping Beauty* or *Cinderella*. In other ballets, there is no story line at all, and the dance and music are used to express moods and emotions, such as sadness or joy. But whether dancing a lead role or simply expressing an emotion, ballet dancers must be highly trained.

The four Little Swans from Act II of Swan Lake

DID YOU KNOW?

The word *ballet* comes from the Italian word *balletto,* which means "little dance." The earliest types of ballet were danced in the royal courts of Italy in the fifteenth and sixteenth centuries. They were called dinner ballets because the dancing took place between the courses of a banquet.

Classical ballet

 lassical ballet (with a small *c*) is based on traditional steps and techniques that have been developed over several centuries. The word *Classical* (with a capital *C*) is also used to describe ballets created in the second half of the nineteenth century.

The fairies from the opening act of The Sleeping Beauty

Putting on a ballet

 utting on a ballet is a mammoth undertaking. First, the company has to choose its ballet. This may be a new version of a classic – with the steps and story interpreted in a different way by the choreographer – or a brand-new, original work. It may be a full-length production or a short showcase piece created for a particular dancer. Whatever the ballet, the dancers, choreographer, and backstage staff prepare themselves for many months of hard work and rehearsals.

How Ballet Began

The first ballets were performed about five hundred years ago. They took the form of lavish spectacles of dancing and singing performed at court for the royal families of Italy and France and for their foreign guests.

Early ballets

The first real ballet, which combined dance, music, and mime in one piece, was called *Le Ballet Comique de la Reine* ("The Comic Ballet of the Queen"). It was staged in 1581 at the French court. The ballet was commissioned by the French queen, Catherine de Medici, to celebrate a wedding. No expense was spared. The ballet lasted for five hours, from 10 P.M. to 3 A.M., and was watched by ten thousand guests.

Woodcut engraving of Le Ballet Comique de la Reine

(left) Ballerina Carlotta Grisi dancing Giselle *in the 1840s*

(right) King Louis XIV in ballet costume

DID YOU KNOW?

La Fille Mal Gardée was the first ballet to show real people and everyday life on stage. Previous ballet stories had focused on gods, spirits, and mythical beings. First performed in 1789, it tells how Lise and her lover, Colas, outwit her mother's plans to marry her off to the son of a rich farmer. The music used today was written in 1828.

A group of waltzers, 1817

FANCY FOOTWORK

Marie de Camargo (1710–1770), known as La Camargo, was the most celebrated dancer of her day. Famous for her brilliance and speed of foot, she is said to have been the first ballerina to master difficult steps such as the *entrechat quatre* (see page 21), previously performed only by men. To show off her dazzling footwork, she daringly raised the hem of her long ballet dress – from floor-length to just above the ankle.

King Louis and the ballet

The first ballet school, the Royal Academy of Dance, was founded in Paris in 1661 by King Louis XIV. King Louis was an accomplished dancer and danced many leading roles himself. Under his patronage France became the ballet capital of the world. One of the school's ballet masters, Pierre Beauchamps, is credited with creating the five positions of the feet that still form the basis of classical ballet today. French is still used to describe the steps and techniques used in ballet.

The first dancers

The very first ballet dancers were courtiers and members of the nobility. Men played women's parts and dressed up in elaborate costumes, masks, and wigs. The first professional female dancers took to the stage in 1681. Among them was Mademoiselle Lafontaine, the first ballerina.

The Romantic movement

The mid-nineteenth century saw the rise of the Romantic movement. Music became more expressive and emotional, as did ballet. The ballets created during this period told tales of spirits, ghosts, and the supernatural, and the ballerina was often cast in a magical, fairy-like role.

A scene from Giselle, *one of the most popular Romantic ballets*

The Classical movement

The Classical movement began in about 1870. A group of French choreographers living in Russia began to work with the Imperial Russian Ballet, creating a new kind of ballet. Classical ballets consisted of three or four acts, with complicated *pas de deux* (see page 22) and solos designed to show off the dancers' technical skills. The most famous choreographer of the time was Marius Petipa (see page 34).

LES SYLPHIDES

Choreographer Michel Fokine created this ballet to music by Chopin in a homage to the earlier Romantic ballet *La Sylphide. Les Sylphides* is a series of dances without a story. It was originally performed in Diaghilev's first season of the Ballets Russes in Paris in 1909.

DID YOU KNOW?

The greatest ballerina of the Romantic period was Maria Taglioni (1804–1884). Her father, a famous Italian ballet master, was determined that his daughter would become a dancer and pushed her hard. She made her debut in Vienna in 1822. Her reputation for grace and lightness of step quickly grew. Every dancer wanted to copy her – there was even a verb, *Taglioniser,* that meant "to dance like Taglioni"! In 1832 she danced the lead in the first true Romantic ballet, *La Sylphide.* It was a triumph. Taglioni retired in 1847 and, sadly, died in poverty.

Petrouchka: *a ballet developed by Diaghilev's Ballets Russes*

BALLET MOVEMENTS

◆ ROMANTIC (ca. 1830–1870) Famous ballets include *La Sylphide* and *Giselle*.
◆ CLASSICAL (ca. 1870–1900) Famous ballets include *Coppélia, The Sleeping Beauty, The Nutcracker,* and *Swan Lake.*
◆ DIAGHILEV'S BALLETS RUSSES (1909–1929) Famous ballets include *The Firebird, Le Spectre de la Rose,* and *Petrouchka.*
◆ MODERN (1930 and onward) Famous ballets include *Who Cares?, Agon, Symphonic Variations, Step Text, Stars and Stripes,* and *Cinderella.*

Diaghilev's Ballets Russes

From about 1909 to 1929, one Russian company reigned over the ballet world. Called the Ballets Russes, the company was founded by the brilliant director Serge Diaghilev. His bold productions revolutionized ballet. Among his greatest protégés were Anna Pavlova and Vaslav Nijinsky (see page 28).

Modern ballet

Ballets created in the twentieth century are known as modern ballets. Many do not tell stories but use dance to express abstract themes and emotions. For example, George Balanchine's ballet *Agon* explores different rhythmic forms. Others are modern interpretations of well-known stories, such as *Manon* or *Cinderella.* Modern ballets use classical steps and techniques in unusual and sometimes exaggerated ways.

The Seven Silences of Salome: *a modern ballet by Olga Roriz*

13

The Ballet Company

A ballet company is a carefully organized team of dancers, choreographers, ballet teachers, musicians, and backstage staff. They work together closely to ensure that every ballet performance is a flawless delight.

The dancers

Most dancers who join a company start their careers in the *corps de ballet,* or chorus. This is a large group of dancers who perform together in close and precise formation. Some *corps* dancers are promoted to *coryphée* and this may be a step to becoming a soloist. Soloists dance important but not leading roles, such as the Fairy Variations in the Prologue of *The Sleeping Beauty.* Very few dancers reach this level. Even fewer are good enough to be chosen as principals and dance the leading roles, such as Prince Siegfried and Odette/Odile in *Swan Lake.*

The principal dancers positioned in the middle of the picture, with the corps de ballet *in lines behind them*

(above) An impressive set design for The Sleeping Beauty

(below) A set painter at work

Becoming a ballerina

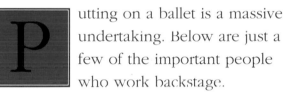

Female principal dancers are sometimes called ballerinas or prima ballerinas. These were originally official titles bestowed by the czar on the finest dancers of the Imperial Russian Ballet. Two great dancers, Pierina Legnani and Mathilde Kschinskaya, were raised to the rank of *prima ballerina assoluta*. In recent times, this accolade was given to Margot Fonteyn (see page 29).

Pierina Legnani

Behind the scenes

Putting on a ballet is a massive undertaking. Below are just a few of the important people who work backstage.

A seamstress preparing dancers' costumes

◆ ARTISTIC DIRECTOR – Selects which ballet to perform, hires the choreographer and designers, and casts the dancers.

◆ COMPANY MANAGER – Looks after the dancers' welfare; organizes tours and salaries.

◆ CHOREOGRAPHER – Creates the steps of the ballet.

◆ BALLET MASTER/MISTRESS – Teaches daily classes and rehearses the ballet.

◆ CHOREOLOGIST (NOTATOR) – Writes down and records the dance steps.

◆ DESIGNER – Designs costumes, lighting, and scenery.

◆ STAGE MANAGER – Coordinates the production, finds props, and makes sure the dancers appear on stage at the right time.

◆ WARDROBE DEPARTMENT – Takes care of the costumes. Most companies also have a wig master and a shoe supervisor.

◆ ORCHESTRA – Works closely with the choreographer to ensure that the music matches the dancing.

Ballet Techniques

Classical ballet is based on techniques that have been developed and refined over centuries. Dancers spend many years learning and perfecting their technique so that difficult steps can be made to seem effortless.

Pull up and turn out

One of the first techniques a dancer learns is how to stand properly. With the back straight, the body is lifted – or "pulled up" – as if by a piece of string. This not only looks graceful but helps the dancer to breathe more deeply and easily. The dancer's legs and feet are turned out from the hips, so that the toes point sideways. This gives the dancer greater flexibility and range of movement.

In a class

To learn ballet, dancers must attend ballet classes. Classes begin with exercises at the *barre,* a long rail running around the classroom wall. It gives the dancers support as they stretch their muscles. *Barre* work is followed by a series of different exercises in the middle of the room that help to improve balance and control. Professional dancers continue to attend classes, even while they are busy rehearsing, to keep their skills and technique in top condition.

PORT DE BRAS

Holding the arms and hands correctly is called *port de bras.* The arms should be relaxed, with the elbows and wrists slightly bent to create a flowing line. The fingers should look natural and relaxed. Together with pull-up and other techniques, the arm positions make a dancer look longer, taller, and more elegant.

A dance student warming up with pliés *at the* barre

En première
(first position)

En seconde
(second position)

En troisième
(third position)

The five positions of the feet and arms

Most ballet steps begin and end with the feet in one of the five positions. These were created by Pierre Beauchamps, Louis XIV's ballet master, to ensure that a dancer's weight is always evenly balanced. The complementary arm positions are designed to give the dancer's body a consistently pleasing line. Nearly all ballet steps incorporate these five basic positions. You will see them being used when a dancer prepares to begin a series of moves, in the middle of a sequence of steps, and at the end of a jump, turn, or pose.

The five basic arm and feet positions

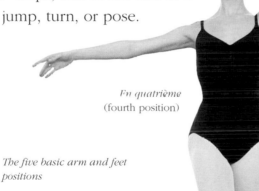

En quatrième
(fourth position)

En cinquième
(fifth position)

The seven movements of dance

Every ballet step is based on seven different types of movement that a dancer's body makes naturally. These are called the seven movements of dance and they are described in French: *plier* ("to bend"), *glisser* ("to glide"), *tourner* ("to turn"), *étendre* ("to stretch"), *sauter* ("to jump"), *relever* ("to rise up"), and *élancer* ("to dart"). The movements are used in steps such as *pliés, battements tendus, glissades, arabesques penchées,* and *grands jetés.*

Relever *("to rise")*

Sauter *("to jump")*

AIRBORNE

Mikhail Baryshnikov could perform the most remarkable *pirouettes* and leaps in midair. He sometimes invented his own steps, such as his turning *jeté,* in which he changes the foot he's going to land on at the last moment, and his legs flash past each other in the air.

The Sleeping Beauty *Act I (above) The Queen pleading with Carabosse, who has cast a spell on Aurora (right) The Lilac Fairy demonstrating her magical powers*

Using mime

Mime is a form of acting without words, a type of sign language in which gestures are used to express emotions and to tell a story. It is often seen in older ballets. A famous mime passage occurs in the christening scene (Prologue) of *The Sleeping Beauty* when first the Fairy Carabosse and then the Lilac Fairy act out Aurora's future. In Act II of *The Nutcracker,* the Nutcracker Prince uses mime to tell the story of how he and Clara came to the Kingdom of Sweets. Another very amusing mime scene takes place in *La Fille Mal Gardée,* when Lise is daydreaming about spending her future with her beloved Colas, unaware that he is watching her every move.

Some Ballet Steps

Next time you see a ballet, watch for some of the steps shown on the next four pages. Different steps are used to portray different actions and emotions. Sequences of steps are repeated and varied. Some steps are danced alone, others with a partner.

Adage steps

dage steps are performed at a slow tempo and require superb balance and control. (*Adage* comes from the Italian *ad agio,* which means "at ease.") One of the most famous *adage* steps is the graceful *arabesque.*

In a simple *arabesque,* the dancer stands on one leg with the other stretched out behind and the arms usually extended.

In an *arabesque penchée,* the dancer leans forward so that the outstretched leg is raised above the head.

In Act II of *Giselle,* for example, Myrtha, Queen of the Wilis, performs several famous *arabesques.* Different styles of *arabesques* are used to express different moods.

Dancers in arabesque

20

Allegro steps

*A*llegro steps are quick, lively steps used for jumping and leaping. Dancers start with *petit* ("small") *allegro* and build up to *grand* ("big") *allegro* when they are stronger and can leap higher. An example of a *petit allegro* is a *soubresaut* ("small jump"). A *grand jeté* is a type of *grand allegro* used for

A dancer perfecting his jumps

travelling through the air. Dancers need very strong leg muscles to perform these dramatic steps and to land lightly, and the most energetic *jetés* are usually performed by the male dancers. *Swan Lake* usually ends with a series of triumphant *jetés* by the male soloists. *Grands jetés* are often used to express strong emotions such as joy, victory, and happiness.

Dancing like a cat

A *pas de chat* ("step of a cat") is a jumping step that imitates the darting action of a pouncing cat. It was created by Marius Petipa for the Dance of the Cats in the first production of *The Sleeping Beauty* (Act III). To perform a *pas de chat* the dancer travels sideways through the air in a series of light, springing movements.

Pas de deux

A *pas de deux* is a step or sequence of steps performed by a male and female dancer working in partnership. The words *pas de deux* mean "step for two." Learning to dance a *pas de deux* takes a great deal of rehearsing together. The two dancers must move in harmony, coordinating their movements and complementing each other perfectly. They must have complete trust in each other, and the male dancer must be strong and confident enough to lift his partner easily and carefully.

Most ballets feature a *pas de deux* at the climax of the story or as the finale. *The Sleeping Beauty* ends with a joyful *grand pas de deux* celebrating the wedding of Princess Aurora and Prince Florimund. In Act II of *The Nutcracker,* the Nutcracker Prince and the Sugar Plum Fairy dance a *grand pas de deux* in the Kingdom of Sweets for Clara. This is the only part of the original choreography to survive. Two famous *pas de deux* are featured in *Swan Lake*. First, the prince dances with Odette, the white swan, and later he dances with Odile, the black swan, mistaking her for his beloved Odette.

A *pirouette,* or "whirl," is a spectacular step in which the dancer spins on one leg. *Pirouettes* can be done quickly or slowly. Whatever their speed, they require great strength, balance, and control. To avoid getting dizzy as they spin, dancers use a special technique called spotting. As they turn they focus on a fixed point – such as a spot on the wall – for as long as possible before flicking their heads around and finding the point again. Some auditoriums have a light at the back for the dancers to focus on as they spin.

Odile dancing with Prince Siegfried in Swan Lake, *Act III*

A *fouetté* is a step in which a dancer stands on one leg and whips the other leg around her body to help her turn. *(Fouetter is French for "to whip.")*

In *Swan Lake* the ballerina playing Odette/Odile performs thirty-two *fouettés* in a row. They were made famous by the Italian ballerina Pierina Legnani in the 1895 premiere of the ballet.

Vaslav Nijinsky and Tamara Karsavina in La Spectre de la Rose, *1911*

Great *pas de deux*

One of the greatest ballet partnerships in recent times was between Margot Fonteyn and Rudolf Nureyev. They first danced together in 1962, when Fonteyn was over forty, forming a partnership based on maturity, quick thinking, and flawless style. Apart from the many classical roles they made their own, they were also the inspiration for many new ballets. The greatest number of curtain calls in ballet history was eighty-nine, given after a performance of *Swan Lake* in Vienna in 1964. The lead roles were danced by Fonteyn and Nureyev.

Margot Fonteyn and Rudolf Nureyev in Romeo and Juliet, *1965*

Other *pas de deux* to watch for

A *pas de deux* is often treated as a showpiece in its own right and is sometimes better known to ballet audiences than the ballet itself. Famous examples to watch for are the *pas de deux* from *The Sleeping Beauty* (Act III), when the Bluebird dances with his princess, and the wedding of Kitri and Basil from *Don Quixote* (Act III). There are some ballets that consist of only a *pas de deux,* such as *Tchaikovsky Pas de Deux* by Balanchine and *Other Dances* by Jerome Robbins.

Shoes and Costumes

A ballerina in a tutu standing on tiptoe is a familiar image – even to those who have never seen a ballet. Costumes and shoes are vital to any ballet and help create the right mood and show off a dancer's technique.

Dancing shoes

Ballet shoes are the most important part of a dancer's equipment. Male dancers wear shoes of leather held on with elastic. Female dancers wear shoes of satin, canvas, or leather, tied with ribbon. Shoes are handmade by special ballet shoemakers and should fit like gloves, not too tight or too loose. They must also be strong and durable – a dancer can go through two pairs of shoes in a single performance.

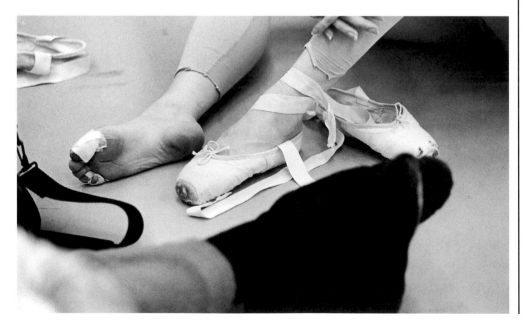

The thirty-two female dancers of the English National Ballet go through 4,080 pairs of shoes every year. They use almost eight gallons (30 litres) of shellac to keep their shoes hard and a mile and a half (2.5 km) of ribbon.

___

In Twyla Tharp's ballet *In the Upper Room* the dancers begin the performance in running shoes, then change into *pointe* shoes later.

Changing pointe *shoes between classes*

En pointe

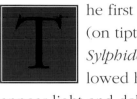

The first ballerina to dance successfully *en pointe* (on tiptoe) was the great Maria Taglioni in *La Sylphide* in 1832. Other dancers quickly followed her lead. Dancing *en pointe* made them appear light and delicate, like fairies or spirits – roles that appeared often in Romantic ballets. But it was not until later in the century, when Italian shoemakers produced "blocked" shoes, that *pointe* work could be sustained for any length of time. Ordinary soft ballet shoes made it not only uncomfortable but also dangerous to stand on tiptoe.

Today's dancers train for several years, and must already have good technique, before being allowed *en pointe*. Their ankles and feet must be strong enough to prevent injury. They wear shoes blocked at the toes with satin and paper, glued together and baked hard, and tied with satin ribbons. Before a class or performance, dancers put rosin or shellac on the tips of their shoes to keep them from sliding on the wooden floor.

Shoes designed for a recent production of Giselle, *based on 1920s fashions*

MODERN FOOTWEAR

In more modern ballets, dancers often wear different types of dance shoes. Male dancers in particular frequently perform in bare feet. In Aaron Copland's modern American ballet *Rodeo*, the men dance wearing cowboy boots!

Male dancers

Men very rarely dance *en pointe* except for special effects. The male pigs in *The Tales of Beatrix Potter*, for example, make tiny animal-like steps *en pointe*. Male dancers need to have great strength and agility to perform powerful leaps and to lift a female partner, and so they concentrate on different exercises in class to build up the muscles needed for their more strenuous work.

A male dancer as Pigling Bland performing en pointe

Dressing the part

Early ballet costumes were based on the dresses worn at court and were heavy with jewels and trimmings, elaborate, and cumbersome. Court dancers also wore heavy shoes with heels. Gradually costumes changed to show off the dancers' footwork and to give them greater ease and range of movement. Beginning in the 1720s dresses became shorter, culminating in the famous classical muslin tutu of the nineteenth century, with its short, stiff skirt and tight bodice. Tutus are still worn in many ballets today. In rehearsals dancers often wear rehearsal tutus to get used to the feel of them before the actual performance.

Certain shades of tutu tend to be associated with particular roles. Good, pure characters such as Aurora in *The Sleeping Beauty* and the Sugar Plum Fairy in *The Nutcracker* usually wear pink tutus. Red and black costumes are associated with more complex or evil characters, such as Odile in *Swan Lake*.

(above) Costumes in storage

(left) Dancers of the Paris Opéra Ballet, 1898, in old-style tutus and bloomers

(top and bottom) Costume designs for The Sleeping Beauty (middle) A costume fitting

Costume design

Ballet costumes, for both men and women, must be comfortable, strong, and easy to dance in. Male dancers often wear tights so that the audience can see their feet and legs clearly. In modern ballets, costumes are used to tell the story and to make characters easier to recognize. The role of the costume designer is very important in the ballet company. He or she works closely with the ballet's choreographer and producer. Top fashion designers, such as Jasper Conran and Christian Dior, are sometimes asked to design the costumes for ballets.

Masks and makeup

Some ballets require elaborate costumes or very theatrical makeup. The dancers in *The Tales of Beatrix Potter* all wear masks made from lightweight plastic, with breathing holes in the cheeks and snouts. In Frederick Ashton's ballet *The Dream* (based on Shakespeare's *A Midsummer Night's Dream),* the dancer who plays Bottom wears a donkey mask. Certain character dancers, who do not need to dance energetically, can be dressed up in elaborate costumes and heavy makeup, such as the Ugly Stepsisters in *Cinderella.*

Mrs. Tiggy Winkle in full costume for The Tales of Beatrix Potter

Great Ballet Dancers

Every so often a ballet dancer appears on stage whose very presence holds the audience spellbound. These are the superstars of the ballet world. They may be famous for their superb technique, musical interpretation, physical grace, or for a combination of all three.

Vaslav Nijinsky in La Spectre de la Rose

ANNA PAVLOVA (1882–1931)
After watching a performance of *The Sleeping Beauty* in 1890, Anna Pavlova vowed to become a ballerina and dance the role of Aurora.

She joined the Imperial Ballet School in St. Petersburg and was given the title ballerina in 1906. She achieved her childhood goal of dancing Aurora in 1908. Pavlova later formed her own ballet company and toured with it worldwide. She is best remembered for her performance in *The Dying Swan,* a solo piece created specially for her by choreographer Michel Fokine.

VASLAV NIJINSKY (1890–1950)
Nijinsky's dancing career was brief but brilliant. Like Pavlova he trained at the Imperial Ballet School in St. Petersburg. In 1909 he starred with Diaghilev's Ballets Russes, where he also choreographed radically original ballets, including *L'Après-midi d'un Faune* and *The Rite of Spring.* Nijinsky's dancing ability made him a legend, even though his career was cut tragically short by illness.

Anna Pavlova in her famous role as The Dying Swan

DID YOU KNOW?

Anna Pavlova danced the role of *The Dying Swan* thousands of times throughout her career. It is even said that the last words she spoke before she died were "Prepare my swan costume."

Margot Fonteyn dancing the lead role of The Firebird *in 1954*

MARGOT FONTEYN (1919–1991)
Margot Fonteyn's talent was spotted at an early age. At sixteen she was chosen from the students at the Vic-Wells Ballet School in London to dance a solo in Dame Ninette de Valois's production of *The Haunted Ballroom*. By the age of twenty, she had danced the leading roles of *Giselle,* Odette/Odile in *Swan Lake,* and Aurora in *The Sleeping Beauty*. She is best known for her long partnership with Rudolf Nureyev, which began when Fonteyn was already over forty years old.

RUDOLF NUREYEV (1938–1993)
A leading star of the Kirov Ballet, Nureyev defected to the West in 1961 while in Paris. The following year he made his London debut at the Royal Ballet, in a dazzling performance of *Giselle.* This was the beginning of his partnership with Margot Fonteyn. From 1983 to 1987, Nureyev was director of the Paris Opéra Ballet. He danced more than one hundred different roles and appeared in the first performance of Kenneth MacMillan's *Romeo and Juliet* (1965). Nureyev created his own spectacular versions of all three of Tchaikovsky's classic ballets.

ARTHUR MITCHELL (1934–   )
Arthur Mitchell became the first black dancer to achieve principal status in an American ballet company. Having trained at Balanchine's School of American Ballet, Mitchell joined the New York City Ballet in 1955 at a time when there were no other black classical ballet dancers. After the assassination of civil rights leader Martin Luther King Jr. in 1968, Mitchell formed a mixed-race company, the Dance Theatre of Harlem. The company is now internationally famous and tours all over the world, performing both classical and modern works.

MIKHAIL BARYSHNIKOV (1948–   )
Another of the great Russian dancers, Baryshnikov studied at the Kirov Ballet School before defecting to the West in 1974 while on tour in Canada. Famous for his superb technique and artistry, he was in demand as a guest dancer throughout the world, but principally danced with the American Ballet Theatre, serving as its director from 1980 to 1989. He now performs with a more contemporary American dance company called the White Oak Dance Project.

Rising stars

Today, young new dancers are making their mark in the world of ballet. The British dancer Darcey Bussell and the French dancer Sylvie Guillem are just two stars who have been praised all over the world for their dazzling technique and artistry.

DARCEY BUSSELL

At the age of twenty-one, Darcey Bussell became a principal dancer at the Royal Ballet in London. Tall and long-limbed, she has received acclaim for her work in ballets such as the New York City Ballet's *Agon,* as well as the roles Kenneth MacMillan created for her in *The Prince of the Pagodas* and *Winter Dreams*. She has also danced the roles of Odette/Odile in *Swan Lake* and Princess Aurora in *The Sleeping Beauty* for the Royal Ballet.

(above) Rehearsing with the choreographer's assistant

(below) American Ballet Theatre's ballerina Susan Jaffe in Études

(left) English ballet star Darcey Bussell as Aurora in The Sleeping Beauty

(above) Augustus van Heerden
in the Dance Theatre of Harlem's
ballet Voluntaries

(right) Artists of the Bolshoi Ballet
in Ivan the Terrible

SYLVIE GUILLEM

Sylvie Guillem was promoted by
Nureyev at the Paris Opéra Ballet
and he choreographed a version of
Cinderella for her, launching her
international career. Famous for her
extensions (she can lift her leg at an
angle of 180 degrees), she enjoys the
excitement of working with choreographers such as William Forsythe
who use exaggerated and extreme
movement.

Choreography

The art of creating the steps and movements for a ballet is called choreography. Most major companies have their own choreographer, usually a dancer or former dancer, who is responsible for creating new ballets.

The ballet mistress (standing) and notator working together in rehearsal

What the choreographer does

The choreographer creates the steps and movements for a ballet, rehearses them with the dancers, and works closely with the set and costume designers and the musical director. The most talented choreographers are in high demand with ballet companies throughout the world! He or she may be inspired by a story, a poem, a piece of music, or even a particular dancer. Alternatively he or she may decide to revive or radically rework one of the classics.

(right) A dancer in arabesque

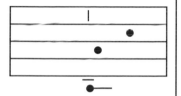

(above) The Benesh notation depicting this position

Writing down a ballet

A choreologer or notator writes down the steps of the ballet, using a system of symbols. Two systems are recognized throughout the world. One is called Labanotation and was developed in 1910, mainly for use with modern dance. The other system, Benesh Movement Notation, was created in the 1940s and is more widely used. Steps and movements are recorded in shorthand form, using symbols written on a five-line musical stave. The dancer's body is divided into five parts (head, shoulders, waist, knees, and lower legs). Each part has its own line on the stave. Three basic symbols are then plotted on the lines to show the position of each body part, to give a three-dimensional picture. These are drawn as if you are looking at the dancer from behind. In a *pas de deux,* each dancer has his or her own stave, just as the different instruments have separate staves in a musical score.

Computer choreography

Because dance involves the whole body moving in three dimensions, recording even a short ballet is extremely complicated. A single minute of dance can take as long as six hours to record on paper. Today sophisticated computer graphics have made the choreographer's task easier. Computer programs can create animated figures to mimic steps, body movements, and stage positions on the monitor. This allows the choreographer to view the stage and dancers from all angles, and to plan productions much more easily.

DID YOU KNOW?

The original notation for the classics *The Sleeping Beauty, The Nutcracker,* and *Swan Lake* was not as detailed as today's systems. However, some modern choreographers have used these original notes to recreate parts of the classic ballets exactly as they were first intended to be performed, for example, Peter Wright's *Snowflake Scene* (1984).

Famous Choreographers

The choreographer not only creates an interesting variety of dances for the ballet company, but also influences its distinctive artistic style. Many of the greatest choreographers were also originally successful dancers in their own right.

JULES PERROT (1810–1892)
Perrot began dancing lessons at the age of ten and was soon appearing on stage. He studied under the great Auguste Vestris who, referring to Perrot's looks, advised him to "turn, spin, fly, but never give the public time to look at you closely"! After a spell as a principal at the Paris Opéra Ballet, Perrot toured widely. In Naples he met the Italian ballerina Carlotta Grisi, for whom he created *Giselle*. He continued to choreograph and teach, in London, St. Petersburg, and Paris, until his retirement. Apart from *Giselle,* his most famous ballet was *Pas de Quatre* (1845), created for the four greatest ballerinas of the day.

MARIUS PETIPA (1818–1910)
The master choreographer of the Classical movement, Petipa created his first full-length work, *Pharaoh's*

Daughter, in 1862. It was a tremendous success. In 1869 Petipa was appointed chief ballet master at the Imperial Theatre in St. Petersburg. From then until his retirement in 1903, he created more than sixty full-length ballets, including *La Bayadère* and *The Sleeping Beauty.* His daughter danced the role of the Lilac Fairy in the first performance of

Artists of the Kirov Ballet in La Bayadère

(above) Male dancers cast as swans in Matthew Bourne's radical version of Swan Lake

(right) Michel Fokine as Harlequin in his own ballet Carnaval

The Sleeping Beauty. With his assistant, Lev Ivanov, he choreographed the first *Nutcracker* and the first successful *Swan Lake*.

MICHEL FOKINE (1880–1942)

Petipa's successor at the Imperial Theatre, Fokine broke away from the formal structures of earlier ballets. His ballets were short, one-act works that told stories through expressive movement rather than formal mime. His most famous ballets were created for Diaghilev's Ballets Russes. They include *The Firebird, Le Spectre de la Rose,* and *Petrouchka*. He worked closely with the two famous dancers Pavlova and Nijinsky.

GEORGE BALANCHINE (1904–1983)

One of the stars of Diaghilev's company, Balanchine left Russia for good in 1924. In the United States, he formed the New York City Ballet and made his career as a choreographer, creating a unique style based on classical technique but with new speed and precision of movement. Although he created his own versions of *The Nutcracker* and *A Midsummer Night's Dream*, many of his ballets do not tell stories but deal with moods and emotions instead. His ballets include *Apollo, Serenade,* and *Stars and Stripes*.

FREDERICK ASHTON (1904–1988)

Frederick Ashton was inspired to become a dancer after seeing Anna Pavlova dance. In 1935 he was invited by Ninette de Valois to join her Vic-Wells company in London. This was the start of Ashton's long association with Margot Fonteyn, who appeared in many of his ballets. Noted for his richness and detail of movement, as well as his ability to tell stories clearly, Ashton is best known for *Les Patineurs, La Fille Mal Gardée, The Dream,* and *The Tales of Beatrix Potter*.

George Balanchine demonstrating steps to artists of the New York City Ballet

Music for the Ballet

Some of the most popular pieces of classical music have been composed for the ballet. Three of the most famous scores are featured on the CD that accompanies this book. But classical music is not the only music used for ballet. Some ballets are set to jazz or rock music.

Early ballet music

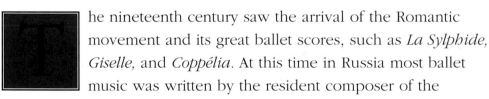

In the early days of ballet, music was provided by the dancing master himself – who also had to be a talented musician. One of the most important composers of the seventeenth century was Louis XIV's court violinist, Jean-Baptiste Lully (1632–1687). He was a great fan of dance. Lully composed more than thirty ballets, replacing the slow, stately music of the traditional *ballet de cour* ("court ballet") with short, fast pieces designed to show off the dancers' speedy footwork.

Resident composers

The nineteenth century saw the arrival of the Romantic movement and its great ballet scores, such as *La Sylphide, Giselle,* and *Coppélia*. At this time in Russia most ballet music was written by the resident composer of the Imperial Theatre. The two main composers were Léon Minkus (1827–1890) and Riccardo Drigo (1846–1930). Written to order, their music was so similar that even ballet experts found it difficult to tell apart. This post was abolished in 1886, paving the way for scores to be commissioned from the leading composers of the day, such as Tchaikovsky.

Igor Stravinsky and Serge Diaghilev together in Seville in 1921

ALL THAT JAZZ

The Nutcracker Sweeties is a one-act ballet created by one of today's most exciting choreographers, David Bintley. The dance is set to Duke Ellington's jazz version of Tchaikovsky's *Nutcracker Suite,* and the costumes have been specially created by top fashion designer Jasper Conran.

Musicians and dancers during a performance

HURRY MUSIC

In the eighteenth century, composers such as Gluck and Mozart wrote important ballet scores (*Don Juan* and *Les Petits Riens,* respectively). But ballet music was generally intended to help the action along, rather like the music that accompanied silent movies. For this reason it was sometimes known as "hurry music."

Music in the twentieth century

The most important ballet composer of the early twentieth century was Igor Stravinsky, who was brought into the ballet world by Diaghilev. Many later composers, such as Benjamin Britten and Aaron Copland, have also written for the ballet, although new full-length scores are often too expensive for most companies to commission.

The orchestra

Early rehearsals and daily classes are accompanied by a pianist. The dancers rehearse their steps and the conductor rehearses the orchestra separately. Performing a ballet for the first time with a full orchestra can be a shock for the dancers and does not usually happen until late in rehearsals. Until the beginning of the twentieth century, the violin – not the piano – usually accompanied a ballet class.

Great Ballet Composers

Many of the world's greatest composers have written for the ballet. In the history of ballet music it is said that Delibes gave ballet its heart, Tchaikovsky its soul, and Stravinsky its respectability.

Peter Tchaikovsky

LÉO DELIBES (1836–1891)
Born in France, Delibes trained at the Paris Conservatoire, where he was a pupil of Adolphe Adam, the composer of *Giselle*. From the age of seventeen, Delibes worked as an organist and accompanist in the Conservatoire. Ten years later he moved to the Paris Opéra and began to compose works for the ballet and opera. While still quite young, Delibes wrote fourteen operettas and helped write the vocal score for the opera *Faust* (1859). His first major work was the ballet music for *La Source* (1868) in partnership with Minkus. It was choreographed by Arthur Saint-Léon, who was the ballet master at the Paris Opéra and himself a great dancer. Delibes followed *La Source* with two complete ballets, *Coppélia* (1870) and *Sylvia* (1876). Delibes's music is famous for its charm, emotion, and brilliant orchestration.

PETER ILYICH TCHAIKOVSKY (1840–1893)
Born in Russia, Tchaikovsky studied at the St. Petersburg Conservatory before moving to Moscow to teach. Composer of three of the most famous ballet scores of all time – *Swan Lake, The Sleeping Beauty,* and *The Nutcracker* – Tchaikovsky enjoyed writing for the ballet and could not understand why so many people considered ballet music an inferior art. He was largely responsible for raising listeners' standards. His music presented new challenges to dancers because of its rich symphonic quality. Tchaikovsky was influenced by Delibes, whose music for *Sylvia* he greatly admired. Many of Tchaikovsky's symphonies, concertos, orchestral suites, and chamber music have made fine ballet scores.

(See pages 50–51 for more about Tchaikovsky and his ballet music.)

Léo Delibes

Sergei Prokofiev

MUSICAL ADAPTATIONS

Many famous pieces of classical music have been adapted to create new ballets. A few of the more commonly performed pieces are:

◆ BEETHOVEN – *The Ninth Symphony* choreographed by Maurice Béjart
◆ TCHAIKOVSKY – *Serenade for Strings* choreographed by George Balanchine
◆ MENDELSSOHN – *A Midsummer Night's Dream* choreographed by George Balanchine; *The Dream* choreographed by Frederick Ashton
◆ ELGAR – *Enigma Variations* choreographed by Frederick Ashton

Igor Stravinsky conducting

IGOR STRAVINSKY (1882–1971)

Born in Russia, Stravinsky was discovered by Diaghilev, who invited him to write the score for *The Firebird*. He became the most distinguished ballet composer after Tchaikovsky, following the success of *The Firebird* with such masterpieces as *Petrouchka, The Rite of Spring, Les Noces,* and *Apollo.* Many of his works were written for and choreographed by George Balanchine. The variety of rhythms in Stravinsky's music is a great challenge to dancers. In 1971 and 1982 the New York City Ballet held Stravinsky festivals, at which the company performed an impressive variety of the composer's works.

SERGEI PROKOFIEV (1891–1953)

Fascinated by ballet, Prokofiev experimented with a number of ideas before his scores for *Chout, Pas d'Acier,* and *Prodigal Son* were accepted by Diaghilev. His two greatest full-length ballets, *Romeo and Juliet* and *Cinderella,* are still enormously popular, although *Romeo and Juliet* was originally rejected by the Bolshoi Ballet because it did not have a happy ending. A third work, *The Stone Flower,* is rarely performed outside Russia.

American western ballets

The American composer Aaron Copland (1900–1990) used traditional folk songs and music in his three "cowboy ballets": *Billy the Kid, Rodeo,* and *Appalachian Spring.* The American musical *Oklahoma!* also incorporates a cowboy-style dream-ballet scene by Agnes de Mille.

Stories from the Ballet

Many famous classical ballets are adaptations of well-known folk stories or fairy tales. Other ballets are based on plays and novels, on historical events, and on bible stories. Modern ballets often do not have stories. They are instead based on themes, ideas, and emotions.

(above) The Kingdom of Sweets from The Nutcracker

(below) The Lilac Fairy expressing her vision of the sleeping Aurora

SWAN LAKE

While hunting, Prince Siegfried falls in love with the Swan Queen, Odette. She is really a beautiful princess, turned into a swan by an evil magician, von Rothbart. At a ball to choose a bride for the prince, von Rothbart's daughter, Odile, appears, disguised as Odette. Siegfried is tricked into promising to marry her. Too late, he realizes his mistake. He and Odette drown themselves in a lake, which is the only way to break von Rothbart's spell.

THE SLEEPING BEAUTY

Princess Aurora is cursed at her christening by the evil Fairy Carabosse. On her sixteenth birthday, Aurora will prick her finger and die. Just in time, the Lilac Fairy changes the spell. Instead of dying, Aurora will fall asleep for one hundred years before being awakened by a prince's kiss. The prophesy comes true and, at the end of the ballet, Aurora's wedding to the prince is celebrated by all the fairy-tale characters.

THE NUTCRACKER

Clara is given a nutracker doll at a Christmas party. On Christmas Eve,

the doll comes to life and takes Clara on an amazing adventure. Together they defeat the evil Mouse King and his army, then travel first to the Land of Snow and then across the Lemonade Sea to the magical Kingdom of Sweets, where the beautiful Sugar Plum Fairy dances.

LA FILLE MAL GARDÉE
("THE BADLY GUARDED DAUGHTER")
Choreography: Jean Dauberval
Music (1828): Louis Hérold
First performed: Bordeaux, 1789
Lise lives with her mother, Widow Simone. She loves a young farmer, Colas, but her mother wants her to marry Alain, the silly son of a wealthy landowner. Lise and Colas meet in secret. On his wedding day, Alain finds Lise in Colas's arms. But all ends happily, and Lise and Colas are married instead.

GISELLE
Choreography: Jean Coralli and Jules Perrot
Music: Adolphe Adam
First performed: Paris, 1841
Giselle loves Loys, thinking he is a poor villager like herself. When she discovers he is, in fact, a nobleman named Albrecht, she goes mad with grief and dies. She joins the Wilis, the spirits of deserted brides who died before their weddings. The Wilis almost drive Albrecht to his death, but Giselle saves him.

COPPÉLIA
Choreography: Arthur Saint-Léon
Music: Léo Delibes
First performed: Paris, 1870
Swanilda, a pretty young girl, is in love with Franz. When Franz sees a beautiful, life-like doll, made by Dr. Coppélius, he thinks she is real and falls in love with her. Dr. Coppélius tries to bring the doll to life. Little does he know that Swanilda has taken Coppélia's place to trick him. When Franz recognizes Swanilda and realizes he really loves *her*, after all, everything ends happily.

Giselle showing her carefree nature and love of dance in Act I

THE FIREBIRD

Choreography: Michel Fokine
Music: Igor Stravinsky
First performed: Paris, 1910
In an enchanted forest Prince Ivan captures the magical firebird. He releases her in return for a magic feather. If he is in trouble and waves the feather, she will save him. Later, while trying to rescue some beautiful princesses, Ivan is trapped by the evil magician Katschey. He waves the feather and is rescued by the firebird.

PETROUCHKA

Choreography: Michel Fokine
Music: Igor Stravinsky
First performed: Paris, 1911
At a fair in St. Petersburg, a showman brings his three puppets – a Moor, a ballerina, and Petrouchka –

Liberty Bell and El Capitan in the pas de deux *from* Stars and Stripes

to life. Petrouchka is killed by the Moor in a fight over the ballerina, but he returns as a ghost to haunt the showman.

CINDERELLA

Choreography: Rostislav Zakharov; also Frederick Ashton
Music: Sergei Prokofiev
First performed: Moscow, 1945
(Ashton version: London, 1948)
Cinderella is left at home while her stepsisters go the ball. Her fairy god-mother appears and changes her rags into a ball gown and diamond slippers but warns Cinderella to be back home by midnight. At the ball, the prince falls in love with her, but she runs off at midnight leaving a slipper behind. The prince vows to marry the owner of the slipper, and after a long search he eventually finds Cinderella again.

STARS AND STRIPES

Choreography: George Balanchine
Music: John Philip Sousa
First performed: New York, 1958
Stars and Stripes captures the spirit of the United States with marching bands, drum majorettes, and cheer-leaders, all dressed in patriotic costumes. For the grand finale, the

Cinderella and the prince finally reunited

Alice before she falls down the rabbit hole

dancers all march together against the backdrop of an American flag.

ALICE IN WONDERLAND
Choreography: Derek Deane
Music: Peter Tchaikovsky
First performed: Southampton, U.K., 1995

Alice falls down a rabbit hole and finds herself in an extraordinary world, where she meets such characters as the White Rabbit, the Ugly Duchess, the March Hare, and the Cheshire Cat. Tchaikovsky's music *Album for the Young* has been newly arranged for this ballet.

Watching a ballet

Before you see a ballet, find out as much as you can about it. Learn the story and listen to the music. When you buy your ticket for the ballet, make sure you will be able to see the stage clearly and try to read the program before the performance begins. It not only tells the story of the ballet but also has information about the music, dancers, and choreographer.

Great Ballet Companies

Today ballet is popular all around the world. Many countries have at least one national ballet company and several smaller regional companies, which perform at home and tour the world. Some of these companies also have ballet schools attached to them.

The Kirov Ballet's corps de ballet in Act II of Swan Lake

PARIS OPÉRA BALLET

The world's oldest ballet school is that associated with the Paris Opéra. It was created in 1713 to provide dancers for the opera-ballets and continues to supply dancers for the company. The Paris Opéra Ballet enjoyed a revival in the 1930s under the guidance of Serge Lifar, a pupil of Diaghilev, and it became one of the world's finest companies in the 1980s under Rudolph Nureyev's direction.

KIROV BALLET AND BOLSHOI BALLET

These two world-famous Russian ballet companies have produced some great dancers, including Rudolf Nureyev and Mikhail Baryshnikov. Both companies grew from the Imperial Russian Ballet company, which danced at the Maryinksy

Artists of the Central Ballet of China in Act II of Swan Lake

COMPANY DATES

◆ 1669 The Paris Opéra Ballet is founded by royal decree of King Louis XIV.

◆ 1829–48 The Royal Danish Ballet flourishes under the direction of choreographer August Bournonville.

◆ 1856 The Bolshoi Theatre opens in Moscow; later it became the Bolshoi Ballet.

◆ 1889 The Kirov Ballet moves to the Maryinsky Theatre in St. Petersburg.

◆ 1909–29 Diaghilev's Ballets Russes take European ballet audiences by storm.

◆ 1930 The Ballet Rambert, founded by Dame Marie Rambert, gives its first performance in London.

◆ 1931 The Vic-Wells Ballet is founded in London by Dame Ninette de Valois; later it became the Royal Ballet.

(right) Voluntaries: *a modern ballet performed by the Dance Theatre of Harlem*

(below) Artists of the English National Ballet in rehearsal

◆ 1939 The American Ballet Theatre is founded in New York.
◆ 1948 The New York City Ballet is founded by George Balanchine.
◆ 1951 The National Ballet of Canada is founded by Celia Franca, a former member of the Royal Ballet.
◆ 1960 The Ballet of the Twentieth Century is founded in Belgium by French dancer Maurice Béjart.
◆ 1962 The Australian Ballet is founded. It had its roots in an earlier company formed by Czech dancer Edouard Borovansky, an ex-member of the Ballets Russes. Its first performance was *Swan Lake*.
◆ 1964 The Tokyo Ballet is founded in Japan.
◆ 1971 The Dance Theatre of Harlem gives its first performance.

Theatre in St. Petersburg. The Kirov is noted for its stylized interpretations of classical ballets. The Bolshoi is most famous for its flamboyant and exciting performances.

NEW YORK CITY BALLET

The New York City Ballet was formed in 1948 by choreographer George Balanchine and Lincoln Kirstein. Balanchine developed a new athletic style of dancing for which the company is world famous. He also established and taught at the School of American Ballet, which continues to train dancers for the company.

ROYAL BALLET

The Royal Ballet, first known as the Vic-Wells Ballet because it danced at both the Old Vic and the Sadler's

Wells Theatres, first performed in 1931. Founded by Ninette de Valois, it quickly acheived worldwide fame with dancers such as Alicia Markova and Margot Fonteyn and choreographers Frederick Ashton and Kenneth MacMillan.

ENGLISH NATIONAL BALLET

Established in 1950 by the great British dancers Alicia Markova and Anton Dolin, the English National Ballet started life as a touring company. It strove to bring classical ballet to audiences throughout Britain, and it soon became an internationally successful company made up of dancers from all around the world. Also known for many years as the London Festival Ballet, the company established *The Nutcracker* as an important ballet in modern Europe.

Dance of the World

Classical ballet originated in Europe, although it is now performed throughout the world. But other countries also have their own traditions of classical dance, often based on themes from religion, history, or folklore.

Indian dance

Classical Indian dance follows strict rules first devised thousands of years ago. Two of the most famous dance styles are Kathakali and Bharata Natyam, both from south India. Kathakali dancers are usually men. They wear elaborate costumes, masks, and makeup to perform dramatic dances based on the great epic poems of Hinduism, accompanied by music. Some performances can last ten hours. From the style of a dancer's costume and makeup, the audience can tell if he is a hero, villain, king, or demon. Red means brave or fierce, green means good, black means evil, and white means pure.

Performing an Indian Odissi dance

Japanese No theatre

Japanese No theatre combines drama, classical dance, song, music, and mime. The performers use their costumes and movements to suggest the story, rather than act it out. No theatre developed from dance dramas performed at temples and shrines in the twelfth and thirteenth centuries. At first performed only on ceremonial occasions in front of an audience of samurai warriors, it later became more popular. There are five types of No plays – god plays, fighting plays, wig plays (in which the main character is female), present-day plays, and demon plays.

INDIAN DANCER

The Indian dancer Shobhana Jeyasingh collaborated with composer Michael Nyman to produce *Configurations* (1988), a six-part dance that combined the Bharata Natyam dance of India with some modern dance techniques.

(below) A traditional costume for the Shanghai Kungu Theatre

Artists of the Tokyo Ballet performing a modernized version of the traditional kabuki dance

Chinese opera

The classical dance of China, which developed in Beijing (Peking), was always linked with opera. Peking Opera, or Ching-hsi, combines drama, mime, dialogue, song, and dance. Each character has its own set of traditional steps, postures, arm movements, and fanciful costumes. Acrobatic movements are often used to suggest violent action. The plays are based on Chinese folklore and history.

Modern dance

Contemporary, or modern, dance was pioneered in the early 1900s by two American dancers, Loie Fuller and Isadora Duncan. Modern dancers use freer, more natural movements and rarely dance *en pointe.* Martha Graham and Merce Cunningham have continued to develop modern dance.

Becoming a Ballet Dancer

Now that you know all about the ballet, it is time to learn what is needed to become a professional ballet dancer. A dancer must have dedication, appropriate physique, a feel for music, and years of training.

Learning the basics

The first step to becoming a professional ballet dancer is to attend ballet classes beginning at about the age of seven. Even if you are not going to be a professional, ballet classes are enjoyable and help improve posture and coordination. The aspiring dancer learns the basic steps and techniques. At ten or eleven years old, promising pupils may audition to go to a professional full-time ballet school. Competition is fierce. The examiners watch students perform simple exercises and also look for the right physique.

A ballet dancer needs to be slim and well proportioned, with a long neck and strong feet. In addition to taking ballet classes, students must study music, drama, choreography, and choreology, as well as academic subjects.

A promising young dance student working on her attitude

Young dancers at the barre

48

A DANCER'S DAY

RD = Rehearsal Day
PD = Performance Day

◆ 7 A.M. Breakfast
◆ 10 A.M. Morning class in the studio
◆ 11:15 A.M. End of morning class **RD** – dancers change for rehearsals **PD** – time for a short break
◆ 11:30 A.M. **RD** – rehearsals begin. The dancers may have to learn a new ballet or rehearse one they already know **PD** – rehearsals for the evening performance begin
◆ 2 P.M. Lunch
RD – rehearsals begin again. Costume fitting **PD** – on-stage rehearsal in costume, with full scenery, lighting, and orchestra
◆ 6 P.M. End of the day
RD – time to go home
PD – preparing for the evening performance. Dancers warm up, then put on costumes and makeup
◆ 7:30 P.M. **PD** – the performance begins
◆ 10 P.M. **PD** – the performance ends. Dancers change and shower, then have a meal and go home to bed!

Dancers waiting in the wings during a performance of Coppélia

Joining a company

Dance students relaxing before their next class

ery few dancers are good enough and dedicated enough to join a company. At the age of six-teen, students begin full-time training at a professional bal-let school usually attached to a company. At least two years of hard training follows, with about seven hours of classes every day. Talented students may be given the chance to perform in minor roles in the company's productions. At the end of their training, the most promising students are picked to join the company. With as many as three hundred dancers competing for one place, many are disappointed. They may audition for other com-panies or choose another type of career in ballet, such as becoming teachers, notators, or set and costume designers. Many dancers retire at about age thirty-five, because of the great physical demands of dancing.

Food and fitness

Because of the need to be slim and fit, dancers have to pay careful attention to diet and exercise. Healthy, high-energy foods such as pasta, rice, and potatoes are good for strength and stamina. Many ballet schools employ experts to give professional nutritional advice.

Tchaikovsky and His Music

Peter Ilyich Tchaikovsky (1840–1893) wrote only three ballets, yet they are considered to be among the greatest ever written. His ballet scores are not simply an accompaniment for the dancers, but superb musical compositions in their own right. At the time his style of music was considered new and radical. Today Tchaikovsky's "symphonic" ballet music is enjoyed in concert halls and on recordings by people all around the world. *The Nutcracker Suite,* for instance, is as popular on cassette and CD as the complete *Nutcracker* ballet is on stage.

The first of Tchaikovsky's three ballets was *Swan Lake,* which he composed for Moscow's Bolshoi Ballet. When it was first performed in 1877, it was considered a flop. The original choreography was poor, the dancers second-rate, and a third of the wonderful score rearranged and ruined. Fortunately the ballet was rescued by Marius Petipa and Lev Ivanov, who completely revised the choreography, and the new version – performed in 1895 – was an instant success. Petipa was so impressed by Tchaikovsky's music that he asked him to write the score for a second ballet, *The Sleeping Beauty.* The great success of this spectacular fairy-tale ballet in 1890 led Petipa to commission *The Nutcracker* in 1892.

Much of Tchaikovsky's other concert music – his symphonies, concertos, and chamber music – has been the inspiration for later ballets, such as Lifar's *Romeo and Juliet,* Balanchine's *Serenade,* and MacMillan's *Anastasia*. His romantic melodies and pulsing rhythms perfectly match the expressive movements of classical dance, making Tchaikovsky a natural master of ballet music.

About *The Nutcracker, Swan Lake,* and *The Sleeping Beauty*

All three of Tchaikovsky's classic ballets provide dancers with a challenging variety of movements and moods, allowing each production of a Tchaikovsky ballet to be a new interpretation. As you listen to the pieces of music on the CD that accompanies this book, try to imagine the style of dancing they are describing. Would the steps be slow and graceful, or is the music better suited to dramatic *jetés* and fast, swirling dances?

Petipa had very precise ideas about the mood and pace of the music he wanted for every scene. In *The Nutcracker,* for example, he instructed Tchaikovsky to make the opening music of the Overture "delicate and mysterious," and the Arabian Dance "cloying and bewitching."

The most memorable musical themes and dances from *Swan Lake* are compiled in *The Swan Lake Suite.* The *pas de deux* (from Act II) is such a perfect example of the type of music used for this style of dance that it is often performed as a showpiece in its own right. Like *The Nutcracker, Swan Lake* contains dances from around the world, such as the Hungarian and Spanish dances. However, Tchaikovsky has cleverly given them a completely different mood from those in *The Nutcracker.*

The magical fairy-tale atmosphere of *The Sleeping Beauty* is different from Tchaikovsky's other ballets. In fact, many connoisseurs consider this ballet to be the most remarkable of the three. Perhaps this is due to its beautiful musical arrangements. But it must also be because the ballet contains Petipa's *Rose Adagio* for Aurora and the four princes – that some suggest was Petipa's greatest work.

Index

Glossary

adage steps Slow ballet steps, such as *arabesques,* requiring great balance and control.

allegro steps Quick ballet steps, such as *jetés,* requiring energy and pace.

arabesque A ballet position in which the dancer stands on one leg while the other is extended behind. Arms may be held in various balancing positions.

attitude A ballet position in which the dancer stands on one leg with the other lifted in front or behind, and arms raised above the head.

ballet company An organization made up of ballet dancers, a director, and all the backstage support needed to produce a variety of ballets. Every company has its own style. Most larger companies tour all over the world as well as perform in their home towns or cities, and some have ballet schools attached to them.

Ballets Russes The Russian company directed by Serge Diaghilev and the ballets this company performed in the early twentieth century.

barre The long rail running around the classroom wall, which dance students use to support themselves while exercising.

battements Beating movements made by a stretched or bent leg.

Benesh Movement Notation The most common system of notation used to record ballet steps in western ballet companies, devised in the 1940s.

choreography The art of composing the steps and movements of a ballet. A choreographer is the person who puts together the different movements that make up a ballet.

classical ballet Traditional ballets that usually tell a well-known story. Such ballets are created with traditional ballet steps and are accompanied by classical music.

Classical movement Ballets created in the second half of the nineteenth century (described as *Classical* with a capital *C*).

entrechat A step in which dancers jump into the air and crisscross their feet. In an *entrechat quatre,* the feet are crossed and uncrossed four times before the dancer lands.

glissade A sliding step that can be made in many directions.

Modern movement Ballets created in the twentieth century. Many do not have a story and use experimental steps and movements.

notator Also known as a choreologist, the person who writes down and records the steps of a ballet, usually at the instruction of the choreographer.

pas de chat A jumping step in the style of a pouncing cat.

pas de deux A sequence of ballet steps performed by a male and female dancer working in partnership.

pirouette A whirling movement in which the dancer spins on one leg.

plié A ballet movement in which the dancer's knees are bent, usually used before or after a jump, the first exercise done at the *barre.*

pointe shoes Ballet shoes with a solid block sewn into their tips, enabling dancers to perform on tiptoe, or *en pointe.*

port de bras The positioning of a dancer's arms.

principals The dancers in the leading roles of a ballet; female principals are sometimes called ballerinas or prima ballerinas.

Romantic movement The ballets created in the middle of the nineteenth century. The Romantic period also describes the style of music at that time, which, like the ballets, was expressive and emotional.

score A written-out piece of music showing how all the instrumental parts of the orchestra should be played. The composer works closely with the choreographer when writing a ballet score.

soloist A dancer who has an important, but not a leading, role.

spotting A dancer's technique of keeping his or her eyes on a fixed point when performing a *pirouette,* to avoid dizziness.

tutu The traditional ballet skirt made from layers of stiff muslin or nylon. The classic version reaches as low as the knees, but the more modern tutu is almost horizontal.

waltz A traditional German-Austrian dance performed with a partner in swift turning steps to music in 3/4 time.

Acknowledgments

Many thanks to Jane Pritchard, Archivist for the English National Ballet, who acted as consultant for the text and picture research. Many of the photographs used are from English National Ballet archives and show members of the company in performance and rehearsal. Thanks also to Kathryn Wade, Director of the English National Ballet School, and to the school's dance students Clara Barbera and Hiroto Saito, who were photographed for this book.

The publishers would also like to thank all those who supplied photographs for this book. The copyright owners are listed below:

Sean Conroy-Hargreaves: front jacket, back jacket (top left, bottom right), 2, 7, 13 (top left), 56
Anthony Crickmay: back jacket (bottom left)
John Starr: back jacket (top right)
Bill Cooper: 6, 9, 18 (top), 19, 20 (middle), 22, 40 (bottom), 42 (right)
Richard Farley: 8, 14
Lebrecht Collection: 10 (bottom left and right), 35 (right), 37, 38, 39
Trustees of the Victoria & Albert Museum: 10 (top right), 11, 26 (left), 29, 35 (bottom left), 36
Patrick Baldwin: 12, 15 (bottom left), 49 (bottom)
John Knill: 13 (right), 27 (left: top and bottom), 43
Sasha Gusov: 15 (bottom right), 21, 24 (left), 25 (top), 30 (top right), 32, 45 (left)
Leslie E. Spatt: 16, 17, 18, 20 (left, bottom right), 33, 35 (top left), 48 (right), 49 (top)
Zoe Dominic: 23 (right)
John Austin: 24 (top right), 26 (right)
Marty Sohl: 24 (bottom right)
Henrietta Butler: 25 (left), 27 (middle left)
Dee Conway: 25 (bottom right), 27 (right), 30 (left, bottom right), 31, 34, 35 (top left), 41, 42 (left), 44, 45 (right), 46, 47
Catherine Ashmore: 40 (top)
Gamba: 48 (left)

Benesh notation, page 33, by Ruth Spivak, English National Ballet School
Benesh Movement Notation © Rudolf Benesh, London, 1955

"A Dancer's Day," page 49, © English National Ballet Education Resources, 1995